When Sexual Harassment Feels Like Prostitution®

By J. Anita Lafayette

When Sexual Harassment Feels Like Prostitution

Library of Congress 2009

ISBN-13: 978-1450507523 (CreateSpace-Assigned)

ISBN-10: 1450507522

Printed in the United States of America by CreateSpace an Amazon.com company. For information regarding special discounts on bulk purchases please contact

Jacqueline_Lafayette@yahoo.com

When Sexual Harassment Feels Like Prostitution

Acknowledgments

This book has been a wonderful experience for me to write. From all the hardships and struggles I have lived through, writing this book is one miracle of many miracles that I have seen. Living with brain swelling, my life is difficult and scary at times, but I face each day with confidence of heart to meet the demands and challenges for that day. I start out each day wondering will I get everything done, which I need to get done that day. On my list of personal things to do, if I get 70-90% done I am pleased. My Higher Power has been faithful each day, when I know I have not earned such amazing grace. I know the power of amazing grace because I have seen grace and I was taught the Highest Power is also Amazing Love.

I had watched a single mother work hard to raise four children and I say thank you for the strength my mother taught me to have. My mother displayed strength up until the day she had passed away. I had admired my mother's strength, but she did not know that I did.

We should find time to acknowledge teachers and mentors and say thank you to them in life. I say thank you to everyone, who has imparted treasures of experience, knowledge, and wisdom through the years. Teachers and mentors help to build character in all of us.

WHEN SEXUAL HARASSMENT FEELS LIKE PROSTITUTION®

Table of Contents

When Sexual Harassment Feels Like Prostitution

Introduction

This book is about you. How do you see yourself? Have you allowed a sexually harassing "boss" to shape your self-worth or have you allowed others to decrease your life's importance? Your inner strength can empower you, as difficulties emerge in your life. I had to have some inner strength, some self value, and some self worth for all the obstacles I have faced in my life. I have looked at battles straight on and my inner strength was my only defense and a good defense, even with brain cancer.

I knew my Higher Power did not create me to be a rug. That was a fact I knew no matter what anyone has done to me. The word rug can be interchanged with low life, door mat, hooker, or prostitute. If I saw myself as something less than a quality human being, I would have allowed myself to become cheapened by poor treatment, by labeling, or stereotypes based on a stranger's value system.

My family did not think I was terrific. Surely, my family should have helped me with my confidence level. Our families are supposed to build confidence into our life. Many times that is not the case. I have developed value in me that only I have shaped by putting words of confidence in my heart. Put a value on your life no matter how rough things have been.

If you let yourself down, pick yourself up. If someone put you down, pick yourself up. If you have fallen, you can get up. You can pick yourself up, hold your head high, and keep moving forward. Holding your head up high and moving forward is a wonderful principle of life. I have been sexually harassed numerous times in over a decade and I still held my head high.

The self-confidence and belief in yourself is a target some people will try and go after; family, friends, the boss and strangers may want to destroy your self-confidence. I am not great or perfect. I just believe in myself, if things are going right, or if things are going wrong. I get up every morning and I like me "first". The more I like me, the better I can appreciate others. The more I value me, the more I can value others. I value my life and I value others. Your inner strength can come from some very good qualities and not be empty pride. I have a high respect for life that my Higher Power has created. I do not like to see people try and destroy innocent or defenseless life. I do not like to see bullying acts or hostile acts thrown at defenseless people. I have been bullied and put into many defenseless situations for over a decade.

I love the sunshine as much as a rainy day. I love me on good days and on bad days. I care for myself, if no one else does. Battling sexual harassment you have to love yourself strongly to not give in and not give up. After a decade of abuse, what did I do with all of that inhumane treatment? I wrote this book for me and I wrote this book for you. I have kept my head up through all of the inhumane treatment. I love life and I am a happy individual. How is that possible? I was not created a door mat and that fact I have known just as well as I know my name. I do not wake up with a surprise name. I do not wake up in the morning with a lesser value on me because another person tries to place a lesser value on me.

One low act is equal to another low act in my book, **When Sexual Harassment Feels Like Prostitution**. I have explained in detail how the two acts can certainly be the same thing in some instances. The low act of sexual harassment does not equal your value in life. In this book, **When Sexual Harassment Feels Like Prostitution**, I am removing the candy label term and I have separated the dirty act of sexual harassment from the value I have for myself. I have also written this book to help you separate the low act of sexual harassment from your higher value in life. While writing this book, I have laughed, healed some emotional wounds, got inspired, plus empowered myself, and I want to inspire others. We can work together to bring about changes in the workplace.

Chapter 1

How Bad is Sexual Harassment?

The CBS Late Show host and comedian, David Letterman was in quite a scandal. On late night television Letterman said, he had received an extortion note for $2 million to pay for a sex scandal cover up or the alleged extortionist would publicly expose David Letterman's "creepy" conduct (1). Nell Scovell, an ex-writer for Letterman quit after five months of working for Letterman in 1990; Scovell claimed the office was sexually charged (2). I am 50 years old with brain cancer, I have experienced sexual harassment for over a decade and I know many offices and businesses are sexually charged. Today, I am giving the sexually harassed females or males, like myself a voice in my easy to carry paperback book, **When Sexual Harassment Feels Like Prostitution**. I have explained some sexual harassment confrontations in detail and the dirty game unleashed on subordinate employees.

How bad is sexual harassment? Sexual harassment has been so bad that my age has not mattered much in the last decade. Sexual harassment described in this book could be anyone in my shoes. How many times in one day does sexual harassment happen in the workplaces across America? Sexual harassment training courses are offered annually at many companies. Still there is a problem that occurs in the workplaces between sexually aggressive individuals and their victims. This book is for me and others, who have endured battles of sexual harassment. I am communicating what I have held in for over a decade. The female victims of sexual harassment are 85% of the Equal Employment Opportunity Commission's (EEOC) statistics and the males are 15% of the reported cases from 2000 to 2008.

Chapter 2

Sexual Harassment Defined

Sexual harassment is the unwelcomed attention given to the sexually harassed victim. The actions of the harasser are not a mishap. The attention is a passionate focus placed upon the victim being sexually harassed. Sexual harassment can be verbal or non-verbal in nature. In most cases, the harasser will repeat his or her sexual harassing behavior.

Types of sexual harassment:

*Sexual comments, jokes or innuendoes

*Suggestive looks, leering, or ogling

*Brushing against someone's body accidentally

*Friendly touches, pats, squeezing body parts, pinches or forced sex.

*Not all actions or sexual harassment are identified easily.

*Flirting, jokes, and innuendos are more difficult to identify.

Chapter 3

Choose Between Paying Your Bills or Sexually Pleasing Your Manager

My feeling during a previous sexual harassment encounter was; am I supposed to choose between paying my bills and the unwanted sexual harassment confrontation coming from a boss? Nobody should be made to feel like they have to decide between paying rent or his or her mortgage and saying yes to the sexual aggressor at work. In that moment to give into sexual solicitation, you have chosen to personally sell out. Sexual harassment on-the-job is not treated like prostitution and in some cases that is exactly the feeling, the option, and the pressure. The boss wishes you; the subordinate would sell out your sex for future payroll checks. The boss knows his or her intimidation tactics threatens your employment; especially over sexual harassment, a big career destroyer for many victims and a small statistical fact. Many individuals, who have been sexually harassed, do not come out on top.

If this book stops one teenager from giving into a forced sex situation with a boss; then sharing my story has been worth it. Sexual harassment, hostile-environment harassment, *quid pro quo harassment, a favor-for-a-favor harassment, this-for-that harassment,* or prostitution on-the-job is now easier to understand. If more teenagers go home and speak to his or her parent(s) about this problem at work; then families will feel stronger or closer. Many parents want the lines of communication open with their teenagers. What manager wants a parent reporting you are prostituting their child? Effective arbitration is needed for teenagers and parents. Teenagers burdened by sexual harassment need goodwill ambassadors waiting for them in the human resources department. No more candy label. My hope is we all are safer at the places we go to work seeking long and rewarding careers.

Chapter 4

The 8:00am – 5:00pm at Work Hooker

I have used the word hooker to define the job position I did not interview for. I have used the word hooker to define the type of pay, which is not normally associated with an accounting career. Most employees in the business communities around America show up to work to fulfill the obligations we were hired to do. The monetary reward received after sex is employment for some sex-selling professionals. I have defined my employment choice as an honest day's work, which is not sexually pleasing a supervisor or manager. The sexual harassment on-the-job and the sex exchange-sale principle is the same for the first shift workers to the third shift workers.

When Sexual Harassment Feels Like Prostitution

What is the "difference between" your work responsibilities have now increased with more accounting responsibilities, more retail departments to manage, more vehicle fleets to manage, more culinary menu items to prepare, more customers to assist, more phone calls to make to clients, or some personal nighttime with the boss at a hotel? The boss guarantees to pay you for handling the extra customers, managing more vehicle fleets, or just meeting the boss at a hotel after work. If you answered the above question with; the boss made all of those requests and there are no differences you are correct.

What are you being paid to do? What was that extra assignment requested from the boss? The hotel sex play was a request. The personal sex favors at the boss' place, or sex favors at your place that helps guarantee your job are all acts of prostitution and not just a nice favor. This prostitution set-up needs to be exposed for the exact name of the game to save future employees many painful experiences.

You cannot believe that you are being placed into that position. You cannot believe your ears, when you hear a manager or supervisor discussing lingerie around you. Since, I have heard underwear discussed at work, I have addressed underwear tactfully in this book. I know I have been shocked by company management's behavior. I am addressing sexual harassment the professionally dressed employees have experienced also. We have endured sexual communication that has clearly pointed to the boss' interest in words or gestures. This topic impacts a broad range of employees.

*Are you at work when the boss has sexually explicit request?

*Are you at a company party when the boss has a sexually charged question?

*Are you allowed to say no or are you able to express no interest in the boss without the fear of retaliation?

*Does the boss make it clear he or she is in a position of authority and at the same time the boss makes a sexual remark or sexual request?

*Are you a prostitute for money or an employee earning a living?

Chapter 5

Hiring People for Sex or Hiring People to Work

A hooker on the street exchanges her body or his body for a few dollars, also. The business of prostitution is normally the sale of sex to obtain monetary payment. The big switch at work is the sexually harassed victim is being solicited by someone, who controls the money paid to you. The manager or supervisor, who authorizes your paycheck every week or every other week, is a little bored and your intimate attention is wanted. The manager or supervisor knows he or she is in a position of monetary power. The manager or supervisor took the job or a promotion to become a boss and to have management authority over a department of people. The boss knows "hiring people" to perform a service for money is involved with the job. The manager or supervisor knows giving raises is a part of the management position. Company management knows he or she is paying you to do a job for the company. To perform sexually for the boss making unwanted sexual advances is a complicated situation. The sexually harassed victim's life can also become more complicated without a paycheck. The sexually harassed victim's life is now more complicated by the boss' aggressiveness or sex play.

How did you handle the boss' sexual request in the past? How will you handle the boss' sexual request in the future? If you are not interested in the boss that will help answer the boss' sexual request. Carry yourself professionally at work all the time, communicate no thank you, and return the conversation back to something related to your job or the company. Feeling like an employee and a prostitute at the same time should never occur in the workplace, but that is exactly the pressure in many instances. I know I had to stand my ground and communicate I am not interested in the boss.

This book is to let you know you are not alone, you did nothing wrong, and this horrible situation is all too common. Today this small paperbacked book can help prepare employees for an ugly emotional battle you might encounter in the future. I personally got so much freedom back by writing this book. I literally wrote on paper I am not the boss' prostitute and that freed me from years of these sexually charged encounters.

This book is now your freedom today from years of sexually charged encounters. Hopefully the information in this book will be your peace of mind for tomorrow's sexually charged encounters with a boss. I am agreeing with you; you are not the boss' prostitute.

Your professional relationships at work are important no matter what your present employment position. If you are a certified consultant, licensed practitioner, a specialist in your field, a highly trained technician, a skilled customer service representative, or a store clerk; none of these are prostitute positions. Why would a boss lower your professional roll?

Chapter 6

The Boss is Offering You a Lower Position, But Better Benefits

I had decided I like to have my check signed by the boss on the corporately approved paper supply used in printing payroll checks. I like my paycheck signed in ink on paper, instead of rolling around in the bed with a boss. Is someone paid better in the office because of intimate sexual relationships with the boss? The complaints heard even from the news media covering sex play at work discusses how the sex play exchanges between a subordinate and a boss could open the door for special monetary pay or special perks. Work pay for sheet play is a dirty little business and no extra miles put on the car to find the prostitute. The prostitute is just down the hall, around the corner, or outside the boss' door. No commute time necessary to find a convenient hooker. An employee's position has been lowered, but the payroll check might improve. You, the subordinate have been insulted and demoted to a sex toy playmate, but you can keep your payroll check coming from the boss, if you sexually satisfy him or her.

A seducer-demander, a power player (4), is a negotiator of the favor system. The boss' intimidating power demonstrated is to keep the victim under his or her guarded control, or under the strict manipulation by the sexual harasser. The victim's life at work is being turned upside down because someone is expressing or demanding sex control and that person is authorizing your payroll check. Sexual harassment is like a weapon your boss can use to mess up your professional career.

Chapter 7

I am Not Interested Leave Me Alone

Why should I have to be subject to sexual harassment? Why should you or I have to be subject to business prostitution? If you are not interested in your manager or supervisor, you should be left alone. How many times does, "I am not interested," still leaves the subordinate in a pressure cooker of an environment? How many times did the sexual harassment go away? How many times did the sexual harassment continue? How many times did you have to leave your job because of sexual aggression from others?

Chapter 8

Knock – Knock it is Favor Time!

The supervisor or manager wants an intimate favor. Knock-knock it is time for a favor to be returned. The sex play is only an intimate favor to show "your appreciation" to the boss paying you. In the mind of the sexual harasser you, the subordinate are returning a nice favor. The boss knows your check brings you satisfaction. The word here is "satisfaction". Your check provides you the opportunity to enjoy some simple pleasures in life. Now "simple pleasures" are a two way exchange. The sexual harasser is thinking there is nothing wrong with seeking "satisfaction" in life and a few "simple pleasures".

Your paycheck does that for you on pay day. Some sexually aggressive supervisors and managers see power and control over money allows them satisfaction and a few simple pleasures, when you "give into" sex solicitation on-the-job. The boss is requesting the subordinate's assistance, so the boss can sleep better at night. The boss needs the subordinate's new special sex duties followed through as a sweet favor being returned.

Chapter 9

Paying People for Sex or Paying People to Work

Prostitution

Something	Quid
For	Pro
Something	Quo

Does the boss know he or she is in a position of monetary payment power? Yes. Do some bosses see payroll as the preferred payment method for sex? The first convenience is financial. The company's payrolls used for sex payments do not hit the boss' personal charge card or the boss' personal bank account. Flashing payroll funds enlarges the managers' and supervisors' playground for sex pleasure activities. The boss hired the subordinate employee for a legitimate position with his or her company and then demands sex favors from the subordinate employee. The second convenience for the boss, he or she does not have to drive his or her car down prostitution row in town, they just come up to the subordinate with the monetary authority sitting firmly on his or her shoulders. The employee is forced to understand the boss' sex desires and the subordinate is just a sexual resource for the harassing boss.

Does the subordinate employee want the boss to continue to handout his or her payroll checks? The boss' money power games for sexual activity needs the spot light turned 180 degrees back on him or her and this book straightforwardly deals with this problem. The boss is using a position of power for sex. The boss is using payroll paid to employees as "leverage against" the employee hired to perform work for the company, as opportunities for sexual pleasure exchanges. I will not be prostituted at work. Yes, I receive my paychecks at work, but I do not say "thank you, boss and I appreciate you, boss," with sexually intimate exchanges. Employees need to understand his or her personal rights are being violated. Sex given for a payment in exchange is the first signs of prostitution and sexual harassment at work. That is not okay.

Chapter 10

No Personal Intimate Appreciation Gestures Returned to the Boss

---

Was my professional respect enough for my boss? No. Too many times my professional respect was not enough. Did I return intimate appreciation to my boss? No. When my boss knew I was not intimately appreciative, the animosity was high in the room. The animosity feeling is a sign of the boss is not a happy camper "sexually" or not a happy "money power" camper. Authoritative power is being used when the boss comes onto you, the subordinate. The "boss hat" is still on his or her head. How dare you not intimately acknowledge the boss' power and accommodate the boss intimately. When the boss returns to give you another chance to like intimate attention, the boss is expecting the subordinate to appreciate the intimate time with the boss. You better appreciate the boss' attention the second time and still you do not.

The boss' ego is now slightly bruised. The boss' power hat has been deflated a bit and this could be embarrassing for the boss. The boss could resent the subordinate employee. The resentment is due to the rejection or a bruised ego. Some people do not like to be rejected. Some people do not like the word no. If this is your boss, the subordinate has another conflict to deal with, the boss' immaturity. Retaliation against the subordinate is an immature thing to do. The act of sexual harassment and retaliation are both illegal.

I have a right and you have a right to say no. Retaliation from the boss is to communicate to the subordinate employee, he or she did not have the individual right to say no to the "boss". Displaying the boss' power by retaliating, after you said no is a reminder he or she is the boss. The boss hat was on during the solicitation. A negative monetary power action (fired from work, your benefits are cut, or you are refused a well deserved raised) displayed by the boss communicates your check was for sexual favors. The boss has scratched your back with a payroll check, now it is time to scratch the boss' back with appreciation by giving sexual favors in return.

You were hired for your sexual abilities instead of your knowledge, education, or employment skills. You were hired to be the manager's employee-at-work hooker. That is a hurtful action and the secret of business prostitution. These types of business scenarios cause tremendous psychological damage to the sexually harassed victim. I am addressing this career destroying action in everyday language for everyone to understand; even working teenagers. At work, the manager turns into a "john" with money to pay you for sexual activities, which are psychologically hurting or insulting to both intelligent adults and teenagers for decades. The psychological attack of being made a business hooker in a moment totally blindsides the victim, traps the employee, and upsets intelligently trained adults and teenagers. The employee is psychologically attacked, economically attacked, and made to fear tomorrow.

Chapter 11

A Favor for a Favor - Quid Pro Quo, the Boss Has a Deal

Prostitution

Something	Quid
For	Pro
Something	Quo

What is hostile-environment harassment, *quid pro quo harassment, a favor-for-a-favor harassment, this-for-that harassment?* Sexual favors are made a part of the employment environment in which managers and supervisors make decisions around either to favor an employee or disadvantage an employee. Sexual favors are a part obtaining your payroll check at work. This is illegal and this is called hostile-environment harassment, *quid pro quo harassment, a favor-for-a-favor harassment, and this-for-that harassment.* The hostile-environment harassment, *quid pro quo harassment, a favor-for-a-favor harassment, and this-for-that harassment* takes place when job benefits are directly tied to the sexual harasser's demand for sex play and the employee servicing the sex demand, which may or may not satisfy the manager now making business decisions based on sex play results. An aggressive administrator promises more money to his or her administrative assistant, if she or he goes out on a date or to bed with the boss. The head administrator threatens to fire the employee, if she or he does not give into the sexual harassment requests made. More retaliation can show up in the form of failing to give a promotion, altering the employee's employment benefits to a lesser degree, and deliberately manipulating job performance information to reflect poor performance; thereby dispensing lower monetary rewards to the employee (5).

"**Quid pro quo harassment**" occurs when "submission to or rejection of such conduct by an individual is used as the basis for employment decisions affecting such individual. **Hostile-environment harassment** may acquire characteristics of "quid pro quo" harassment, if the offending supervisor abuses his authority over employment decisions to force the victim to endure or participate in the sexual conduct." (e).

PROMPT ACTION: If Human Resources guaranteed the sexual harassed victim an equal job position, or (e.g.), income for 18-24 months after reporting a verifiable sexual harassment claim in writing, this action communicates to the employee, his or her economic safety is number one, re-establishing sexual acts are not required for company benefits, and the employee is highly valued. If Human Resources (HR) intervened as an Ambassador to reassure the **employee's value,** this would be a huge act of non-threatening arbitration. I believe the HR department can be goodwill ambassadors. This type of action could speak volumes in the court system. Motivate employees to seek HR immediately. A less hostile workplace is created and Human Resources' actions help to return some dignity of the sexually harassed employee. Equal opportunity and humane treatment are big agendas at many companies. If the employee signs a release with the 18-24 month employment guarantee, the company will have saved money from damages and legal costs.

If companies enacted aggressive non-threatening arbitration, how could the companies end up in the court system over sexual harassment over managers or supervisors? New frameworks for sexual harassment and prostitution, which are non-threatening arbitration, will help create a less hostile work environment. The protected employee would still have to meet the expectations of job performance like quality work and being on time, if the employee decides to remain with the company.

Chapter 12

Sharing Special Events

How many times did you remember the boss' wedding anniversary or employment anniversary date? How many times did you remember the boss' birthday and brought in a cake? How many times did the staff buy the boss' lunch as a surprise? All of these kind gestures are to build up a positive relationship and show respect to the boss. These types of gestures are the only expectations a boss should have at work from his or her subordinates, besides the subordinates doing their job. The boss should not expect any special intimate sexual favors from a subordinate employee.

Chapter 13

My Payroll Check is Being Invisibly Dangled Over My Head

If the sexually harassed victim's paycheck is invisibly dangling over his or her head during harassment, that is a very real feeling. The sexually harassed victim knows where his or her payroll check is coming from. The payroll check is coming from the person of power propositioning you. Your check is dangling over your head is a reasonable thought, due to the possibility of losing your job. Those moments are times of total humiliation for the sexually harassed victim, who does not want a personal relationship with the boss. Sex playing at work is a dirty little game.

Chapter 14

The Boss Owns My Toothbrush and My Underwear, Too!

Some supervisors and managers see that you take pride in how you present yourself. You are neatly groomed, maybe wear a nice fragrance, and you dress moderately; not cheap. Moderate apparel is still fair game to the boss. Not every person, who is sexually harassed, is dressing cheap and that dressing cheap stereotype needs to be changed. The boss sees a plate, a delicacy, and a future satisfaction opportunity. The unique acquisition of the employee is a sex resource for personal satisfaction. The sex play gratification can be communicated in various approaches. Maybe the boss is touching you; maybe you are receiving personal compliments with serious communication of interest; maybe you are experiencing the flirtatious game of footsy; maybe you are receiving long stares that send chills down your spine; maybe you are asked out for personal time with the boss, or maybe you have received a pinch on the cheek.

I have also experienced the pressure of what I am wearing is conveniently being taking care of by my payroll check. Sometimes you feel like there is a fire breathing dragon in close proximity. The boss is using aggressive harassment and intimidation. Of course, the company is paying my wage, which takes care of my meals, the roof over my head, any perfume I might buy, and make-up. The hounding boss likes the adornment of what the employee wears, the trimmings, or the sex plate standing in front of him or her. Your personal best of moderate apparel presented at work is sponsored directly by the person authorizing your payroll check. The nicely dressed "sex plate" makes the supervisor or manager feel really good that he or she could accommodate the subordinate to basic conveniences, what you wear, what you own, and where you live.

Chapter 15

The Boss' Intimate Future Expectations

In the boss' mind, the sexual aggressor there is no apparent separation from my payroll check was "earned" for the work I had performed on-the-job; to the boss pays the subordinate for future sex favors. The subordinate is a tasty sex plate and the particulars that make up the subordinate's life, the boss wishes to "cash in" on. The subordinate is made to feel owned by the person, who authorizes his or her check. Working is based on a system of sweet conveniences for the supervisor or manager.

When Sexual Harassment Feels Like Prostitution

You are made to feel like you are working for the boss' personal sex pleasure and not an employee earning a financial standard of living. Writing this book brings back feelings of total humiliation to the surface, again. Total frustration, anger, and humiliation is felt when I got dressed, sprayed on perfume, and combed my hair in the morning. Am I supposed to do less preparation in getting ready for work? I know many times I have preferred not to wear make-up to work because I did not want to add fuel to the sexual harassment environment. In the 21st century world of monitoring your neighbor and employees, tracking is more annoying. A hounding boss demands you slip into your underwear with the boss' future sex needs in mind. A special sex playmate expectation is made at work. The boss has made his or her expectation known for future intimate playtime.

The manager or supervisor can sit across from the subordinate employee breathing like a sex dragon. The subordinate feels like a "sex plate" or chattel property, paid by a payroll check. The professional relationship between the boss and the employee has been changed. The business environment is now a sexual harassment den and a superior can feel very comfortable expressing sexual needs, while the subordinate employee is very uncomfortable.

Chapter 16

No Stress Outlet for the Sexually Harassed Victims

Writing this book is a way of having an outlet from all the unwanted attention from managers or supervisors in the workplace. I wanted to have a way of saying I do not want my payroll check associated with sex favors for the boss. I could step away, if I was made to feel uncomfortable. I have wanted to verbally say, I am not here for that position, the boss' sex mate. I could not say those words to the boss.

This book is just one voice finally getting an opportunity to say the sex exchange-sale game for my payroll check was not the line of work I had applied for. I could not say that to any supervisor or manager. Should every manager and supervisor read this book? Companies are holding supervisors and managers accountable for many company policies. I just believe the sexually harassed victim's voice needs to be heard, after being humiliated. There is not an outlet to deal with this battle, not unless you stay at the psychiatrist's office or use up all of your employee assistance program sessions at work. Just one time of being sexually harassed is enough, but encountering this type of ignorance repeatedly is unnecessary.

Chapter 17

Human Resources the Company's Process

Read your employee's manual regarding how to handle sexual harassment at work or the special pamphlet on sexual harassment. You can go to human resources (HR) to address the issue. I have worked for many companies in over a decade. With so much sexual harassment going on, the need for me to visit HR was too repetitive. I have asked myself this question: How many trips to human resources does a person have to make in one's working career? The answer to that question is however many times it is necessary to speak with someone in human resources or call the employee's anonymous tip line. The proper channels must be taken in the business world. Sometimes, the sexually harassed victim feels cornered. The fear of missing income from losing a job happens quite a bit. I know I have endured sexual harassment longer in order to keep a paycheck coming. Many sexually harassed victims have refused to quit work.

Chapter 18

I Have Been There and Maybe You've Been There

This book is a reflection from over 20 years of working and more than a decade of dealing with sexual harassment at work. This book is for you that have been there and have gone through sexual harassment. I am not trying to scare anyone about future confrontations. The book is not about putting the manager under the microscope, but what supervisors and managers have done. I have been made to feel uncomfortable numerous times by a supervisor or a manager at work. I had many years of working at various companies and never had a problem. I was working with male supervisors and male managers, who never made me feel uncomfortable. The years following turning 38 years old have been hell for me and I am 50 years old, when I sat down to write this book. What am I feeling? Enough is enough.

Chapter 19

The Stress and the Threat are Real for the Sexually Harassed Victim

---

Through no fault of the person being sexually harassed, the pressure from the possible loss of income is very real. The pressure turns into stress. The pressure can become a loss of rest at night; lying awake from worry. The sex play at work with your income associated with the sex play is real. Your supervisor or manager harassing you knows the confrontations are not always wanted, but the boss does not care about your peace of mind. The boss cares about his or her sexual needs, which is a pleasurable state of mind for the boss.

Chapter 20

Some People May Give into Sexual Advances at Work

A subordinate may have felt satisfying a supervisor or manager in a sexual way is worth the peace of mind. The subordinate employee maybe interested in avoiding the pain of disappointing the boss and possible retaliation from not being a sexual source for the boss. Many people feel attention for the opposite sex is always pleasurable, even if the source is a boss. A subordinate may want the extra attention and getting the extra attention from the boss is satisfying and flattering, but not all of the employees find that sex play flattering. Some feel that type of business engagement is debasing oneself. Debasing me was not an option.

Chapter 21

The Negative Impacts of Sexual Harassment

Has my life been negatively impacted from sexual harassment? Yes. I had to start over after sexual harassment confrontations at work. Did my income take a hit over the course of my career because of sexual harassment? Yes. The process of starting over compared to continuing at work adds up in dollars and cents. How long does it take to find another job? How much does your resume suffer? Candidates answering any gaps of employment on an application address another impact the sexually harassed victim remembers. Gaps in employment are frowned upon in the big picture of a really good candidate.

When Sexual Harassment Feels Like Prostitution

Leaving a job because of sexual harassment fills a life with uncertainty.

Have I started over? Yes, I have. I have started over courageously, but the journey could have been better, if sexual selfishness was removed from the workplace. Some people rebound wonderfully after sexual harassment problems. In the total number of the sexually harassed victims starting over, we all do not regain momentum. That is just the statistics of my journey. Running into sexual harassment repeatedly benefits the aggressors far more than the sexually harassed victims.

You the victim did not create the sexually hostile work environment. The sexually harassing boss creates the sexually hostile environment or a work-peer sexually harassing you. The pain of being rejected, if the boss is seeking the attention was also brought about by the boss' actions. Retaliation is ugly and painful, but the sex aggressor initiated the sexual exchange scenario at work and then reacts negatively to a subordinate, who has a right to not be interested in the boss.

Chapter 22

The Job Loss Recovery Process Burdened by the Sexually Harassed for Decades

The sexually harassed victims have been enduring longer recovery periods collectively for decades. If the sexually harassed victims endure a longer period of discomfort, maybe the supervisors or managers should read picking up a sexual situation for monetary power payments (prostitution) is not acceptable behavior and quite illegal. Managers or supervisors should have access to material regarding money payments and sex received is prostitution, even at work. The truth needs to be read by the sex dealing operators, called supervisors and managers, who are actively seeking sex from subordinate employees.

Prostitution does not look good on the employee's work record. A sexually harassed subordinate employee let go from a job does not look good, either. How many sexually harassed victims have shouldered the losses of jobs for decades? Hold the sex solicitors accountable for "destroying" lives and are hiding behind the management titles. It is time for a new dialogue regarding sexual harassment, prostitution, and monetary positions of power used to destroy the livelihood of thousands of subordinate employees.

Chapter 23

Starting Over Looking for Work

To everyone that recovers from being placed in that position; I say wonderful. Why should I today even think or have the slightest concern of future confrontations of sexual harassment? (Fictitious names and examples next) I did not foresee sexual harassment occurring at the A&B Corporation, but it did. I did not foresee sexual harassment occurring at the XDX Corporation and it happened again. I did not foresee sexual harassment occurring at the ZSC Corporation and it happened again. I began to feel like the model sex-mate at work for company management. I dress moderately and did not wear make-up to work 90% of the time. Sexual harassment is more about the aggressive nature of one person to dominate over the victim. It was an ugly and dirty game at work. Sexual harassment had been repeated too many times and it was back to back in some cases. I surely do not know if sexual harassment will show up at XYZ Corporation in the future. I cannot worry about sexual harassment, but yes the thought does come up. I have seen more sexual harassment in the last 12 years, than I had seen before that time. My younger years had less of a problem. Certainly, the problem I have described is more likely to happen in your first 15 years out from college or high school. Surely, the problem of sexual harassment is a problem for your youthful years. No, the problem of sexual harassment has been more of a problem after I had turned 38 years of age.

Experiencing sexual harassment and starting over being a bit older definitely steals from crucial years. I had to start over more after the age of 38, when I could have settled into a position. The statistic of how much more of an impact made is real. If a person like me is single, the problem is 200% more of an inconvenience. The majority of the time the sexual harasser does not deal with the same losses as the sexually harassed victims. Getting away with sexual harassment has been in the harasser's advantage for decades. Start over; I have done. Ignore the sexual harasser; I have done that too. I have done all that I have known to do.

Starting over looking for work is a painful process. A sexually harassed victim can be emotionally or financially fragile and not want to lose an income, the benefits, and the security. Maintaining his or her financial security might be the priority of a sexually harassed person. Teenagers and adults are over powered by sexually wanton bosses because their employment and economic security are threatened. Employees are first threatened by the sexual confrontation and then threatened next by the possible loss of a job.

Chapter 24

Where Does the Benefits & Perks Come From for the Sex Exchange System?

Sleeping with the boss is satisfying for some and the boss' sexual needs are fulfilled from an employee, the sex mate resources found at work. Where does the extra money and benefits come from to add a perk or two for sexual pleasure fulfilled? Does the money come out of the manager's or supervisor's pocket directly all of the time? The **workplace suspicions** are pay perks are added to the employee, who is sleeping with the boss. If someone is being paid extra for sexually satisfying the boss, the money is coming from the company's

account. This type of business is over and beyond the boss'
birthday cake and a card for the boss' anniversary.

Chapter 25

I am Not for Sale

The people working a prostitution arrangement are socially ready to sale sex satisfaction for cash and possibly other bonuses. I do not go to work socially ready to sell-out myself for extra cash on my raise or a special bonus. I have focused on a legitimate career based on a totally different value system. I have not been willing to sell me or lower my value system. Today, I written this book to express all the other real pressures and emotions I have kept to myself. I can speak up for myself and say I will not be an employee for a dirty-favor exchange system on the company's books; supposedly only known by the manager or supervisor with aggressive monetary power.

When Sexual Harassment Feels Like Prostitution

When I could not say sexual harassment from the boss feels like an invitation to prostitute me, I decided to say it in a big way in writing this book. I am not selling myself today. I did not sell myself yesterday. I have a different value system that has been worth keeping. I am not for sale feels good to me, but the setbacks from sexual harassment of course was not a pleasure.

*Boss animosity due to rejecting the boss' sex pleasure

*Boss retaliation due to rejecting the boss' sex pleasure

*Loss of my job due to rejecting the boss' sex pleasure

*Loss of income due to rejecting the boss' sex pleasure

This book was written to stop those four points from impacting my economic security, which was repeatedly under attack. How many more times could I endure those things happening to me? Just sell my need for economic security by sexually pleasing a boss. I saw the negative economic impact that had to stop in my life and my only option was to write this book. I was being confronted too many times and I have brain cancer.

Chapter 26

Harsh Statistics - What are Sexual Harassment Studies Showing?

A commentary on statistics:

When money power and sexual desires meet up, there are few options in dealing effectively with these difficult situations. Workers like me are limited in avenues to take [6].

- Sexual harassment affects for some Fortune 500 companies with losses are $6.7 million per year just in absenteeism, changes in productivity, and turnover.

- Legal settlements average $450,000 in sexual harassment lawsuit cases.

- A superior is one out of two incidents of sexual harassment.

- Approximately one out of two victims does not report sexual harassment for fear of being punished or not believed.

- Sexual harassment comes in these forms at work also; letters and phone calls.

- Physical symptoms that some women suffer from are debilitating stress reactions, including depression, and headaches [6].

The negative impacts made on the sexually harassed victims are significant. I suggest to my readers to find more books on sexual harassment. This book explains the examples of prostitution/sexual harassment at work in detail.

Chapter 27

Maybe Others Need to Get the Weight Off His or Her Shoulders

I hope this book circulates to businesses everywhere. I hope this book shakes up the workplaces from the corporate offices to the factories. The timid and bullied employees will read the emotional scars are huge. I have taken time to put the offense into one word, prostitution. If anyone asks about this little book, tell them this little book is hilarious. I have used my humor, but my topic is serious. The funny little book is a must read book. Maybe this book is good for sexual harassment training and seminars. Maybe this book is good for the employee's breakroom. I would have loved a copy of this book in the offices I had previously worked in. Instead of holding the stress of the dirty sexual harassment game in, or just seeing a message on the employee's board in the employee's breakroom stating sexual harassment confrontations can be perceived as sex solicitation like prostitution based on money payments for sex favors; this would have been nice. Why? It is time to expose the sex dealers at work. It is time to expose the business prostitution at work.

My goal is to lessen the number of job losses for the sexually harassed employees. My goal is to urge companies to organize aggressive arbitration frameworks to reassure frightened workers, his or her job security is important. Re-establishing job security in the middle of a painful process will help remove some of the stress from the prostitution elements experienced from an encounter of sexual harassment with a boss. The employee needs his or her job. What were they asked to do to save their job security?

I have overcome homelessness a few years ago and I had worked my way off the streets. Could I overcome that again? Employment is very important to the safety of the working class.

Chapter 28

The Sexually Harassed Victim Know He or She Has Been Poorly Treated

How many of the sexual harassers complain of poor treatment? How many sexual harassers feel the effects of his or her income stopping totally? How many sexual harassers feel satisfaction, when the sexually harassed victim is gone, transferred to another department, or left the company? The sexual harasser has his or her check coming on the next pay period. The sexual harasser has his or her medical benefits continuing. The sexual harasser knows his or her rent or mortgage payments are still covered and guaranteed after harassing someone on many occasions. The future monetary comfort had stopped for the sexually harassed victim in many situations. That is the crime that only one person understands, the sexually harassed victim. I have tried to pursue legal actions one time and I was made to look like a fool because I did not have a list of witnesses, who saw the sexual harassment occur. The sexual harasser got away clean. I had lost a job to only make another statistic.

Sexual harassment is not just harassment. Sexual harassment is prostitution. Jobs are being lost because of prostitution in the workplace. Employees are losing sleep because of prostitution in the workplace. Employees are made physically and emotionally ill because of the stressful prostitution elements at work. Prostitution is not an acceptable organization in our culture. Why are the elements of prostitution in the workplace? Now someone is calling attention to this problem in basic and easy to understand language. Sexual harassment in the workplace also means prostitution.

Chapter 29

A Wolf Demanding Sex is Sitting in a Manager's Chair

Many times, I have felt like I was supposed to be some kind of "boss property" and I supposedly had no choice to my independence because I had received a payroll check. I am shocked by how many bosses are sexually hostile. Those days of the naïve subordinate employees, who do not have a right over his or her sexuality will be less because I am taking the candy label off the term sexual harassment. Wolves in sheep's clothing are operating out of company offices across this country. Managers are leveraging sex from employees by using the company's payroll systems, as bargaining chips, which allows bosses the ability to act effectively to get subordinate employees into bed with them (superiors with authority). This crime is repeating in cities and businesses all across this country and needs to stop. Sexual harassment is the person-to-person illegal dealing candy store operating at work. Hostile-environment harassment, quid pro quo harassment, a favor-for-a-favor harassment, and this-for-that harassment are not explained as prostitution on-the-job here in America. I am writing these books to explain sexual harassment in simple English and straightforwardly. The sex dealing bosses may have to be more professional and stop sex hustling subordinate employees.

Chapter 30

What is My Payroll Check For?

This subordinate employee's view from my payroll check to **"the services I had rendered"** needs another good look from a different angle. My perception from my application, to my employee orientation, and my job description has only one intention; I am paid to perform my job description. Why would a manager think my payroll check was for the boss' sex favors? Hustling management's "money power" over the head of a "subordinate for sexual encounters" by the boss is prostitution using the earnings of corporate America. The boss is letting you know, the subordinate employee is a convenient hooker at work.

When Sexual Harassment Feels Like Prostitution

Some managers and supervisors do not let you forget you said no to their previous sexual advances. What is my payroll check for?

Today, I sit here with brain cancer and wrote out this book. I have endured sexual harassment and I have cancer. I have decided to write enough is enough. Life has not been easy, but I have lived each day courageously.

If present and future managers or supervisors read this book and understand the horrible situation of sexual harassment better and this information helps managers make positive interpersonal changes now and into the future; then sharing my story has been worth it. If fewer employees leave his or her job over sexual harassment, this directly impacts future employee's seniority at work. Longer careers mean experiencing the company benefits for employees with longer tenure. If supervisors or managers see the need to be professional role models or leaders to a greater degree; then sharing my story was worth it. This book is looking for leaders to be transparent and leaders, who are professional role models, also.

Chapter 31

Employee Safe Zones

What will tomorrow be like for thousands of employees at work not having to worry about sex solicitation coming from the boss on company time using company money? You and I can go to work and not have our payroll check used as a sex leverage exchange system by the boss. What is my payroll check for? It is time to ask the boss a new question. Do you know your position of power, payroll authorization, and payment can be seen as solicitation for sex; when you sexually harassed a subordinate employee? If prostitution is a real feeling for the subordinate employee, it needs to be made clear to bosses that solicitation for sex and a monetary reward associated are the same anywhere. Some people need help separating a payroll check from a sex favor system of operation. The boss needs to know this fact. It is time to separate the payroll check from a prostitution feeling system on corporate America's payroll books. Dealing with power, money authority, and the sex politics more firmly can have a positive impact in the end. Fewer people will leave his or her places of employment, due to sexual harassment and that statistic is worth changing; to make working a pleasant situation for people like me. Enough is enough. Sexual harassment is not fun.

Some bosses may be deterred in the future from sexually harassing other employees because of the nice goodwill package offered to the sexually harassed employee and the boss has an incentive to avoid having prostitution written in his or her employee file. Both the company wins and the sexually harassed employee wins in the end. Our culture frowns on prostitution and the sexual harassment candy label has been removed. Many bosses will change from sexual harassing staff to building respect as a manager. Positive leadership is a better choice.

Chapter 32

Write Down Everything, Record Confrontations, Talk to HR, Family, Friends and the Police

---

The subordinate employee needs to concretely establish the boss' unwanted flirtatious behavior and other outward gestures. For your safety, protection, and legal evidence document the flirting behavior. Write down the sexual harasser's name, what was said or done; the place where the sexual harassment had occurred; the date and time of the sexual harassing. Keep a record of all the events. I have read stories about employees, who have been stalked by his or her boss, too. If you are being stalked by your boss or anyone contact the police.

When Sexual Harassment Feels Like Prostitution

Communicate clearly, firmly, and professionally you are not interested in the boss. Do not let the extremely flirtatious and tongue-hanging compliments from the boss go ignored. Your standard of living is being targeted by the sexual harasser. Your personal safety is indirectly threatened and your employment history is being targeted by the boss; if the subordinate does not dish out some sex favors to the boss. Your options are to communicate with HR and maybe contact your company's anonymous employee helpline. Talk to family and people you know away from the job about your concern over how you are being treated at work.

Many teenagers do not report harassment occurring from his or her boss. Some statistics are reporting over 30% of teenagers are enduring sexual harassment at work. Teenagers are also being physically touched and verbally abused by supervisors or managers. If adults are forced into having sex with bosses, what is happening to teenagers? Do teenagers need to know they are being prostituted on-the-job? Every teenager needs to be empowered and informed that prostitution on-the-job is illegal. No more candy label; illegal sexual harassment is also illegal prostitution in some cases.

Chapter 33

Managers Can be Sexually Harassed by Employees

Managers can be sexually harassed by employees, but this is rare. Sexually aggressive employees can also target his or her manager or supervisor. The ability to want to destroy someone's life is a two-way street. Management has ways to deal with an employee, whose behavior is not professional, but is forcefully sexual around the boss. The company has sexual harassment policies and procedures from letters of warning to termination of employment. Protecting the reputation of managers and supervisors is important. If a manager is behind closed doors with a subordinate, companies can audio or video tape meetings with managers and subordinates. The savings from fewer sexual harassment cases in the court system will save corporations hundreds of thousands of dollars to millions of dollars. Audio and video taping closed door meetings can save pennies on the dollar on legal battles; when compared to court fighting sexual harassment. Manager's offices can have a discreet sign on the wall stating "meetings are audio and video taped" for the employee's safety, or the manager's safety. Neutralizing or diminishing the occurrence of sexual harassment will save everyone hardships, time, and money.

Lowering company damages in the court system means better raises, more company functions, and bonuses. Less stress at work means employees are motivated and happier. One large sexual harassment lawsuit impacts the whole company.

Chapter 34

Companies, Stakeholders and Victims are Penalized Due to Sexual Harassers

The company is in business to provide goods and services to the customers and clients. The company loses money in legal costs because of sexual harassers. Holding the manager or the supervisor harassers more accountable legally for the solicitation of sexual pleasures on-the-job is turning the negative impacts around 180 degrees. The company is refereeing sexual harassment situations with lawyers and the courts. A boss' soliciting for sex on-the-job needs another legal look. The victims need relief from these sexual harassers. I believe companies need more legal recourse to go after supervisors or managers for the act of soliciting subordinate employees for sex.

The subordinate has less legal back-up, the subordinate's guards are down, and many subordinates like me are being made to bear the brunt of the system of sexual harassment. The subordinate employees at work cannot fight the manager or a supervisor in a sex and money leveraging system. I did not want to go after my employer necessarily; I have wanted the sexual harassment to STOP. Enough is enough. Many victims would agree with me; we want the sexual harassment to stop. I have wanted to enjoy the businesses I have worked for and the sexual harassment prevents employees like me from enjoying the place we spend most of our time.

I have brain cancer and I am the least able to defend myself. I have hidden my brain cancer from my employer, so I could work and provide a standard of living for myself. I have gone to work and I carry the burden of my health privately. To go to work with cancer and still have to deal with sex selfish people in supervisory or management positions is too much. Looking in the eyes of sex selfish individuals and I have cancer, I see psychologically sick people. I see selfish people. I got up and went to work courageously to earn a living, to mind my own business, and I have been sexually harassed horribly at work. Enough is enough. The sex driven supervisor or manager will go after anyone. It is horrible to run employees off from going to the place he or she was hired to work. I have been hounded. I have been living with cancer. Sexual harassment is cruel. Brain cancer is cruel, too. The two together are unbearable.

Chapter 35

Numbers Reported Cases with Equal Employment
Opportunity Commission (EEOC) 2000-2008

If the number of cases reported to EEOC were just 20-50%
of the total number of people, who have been sexually harassed,
in the workplaces of America, this could be thousands more of
sexual harassment cases unreported in the last eight years. Does
everyone, who has been sexually harassed, report the incident
with EEOC? If I have been sexually harassed 10 times and
reported one case, the numbers are very low. People do not take
time off from work and go report every sexual harassment
problem, plus many companies are dealing with sexual
harassment situations internally.

Sexual Harassment Charges (7)

EEOC & FEPAs Combined: FY 2000 - FY 2008

	Y 2000	Y 2001	Y 2002	Y 2003	Y 2004	Y 2005	Y 2006	Y 2007	Y 2008
eceipts	5,836	5,475	4,396	3,566	3,136	2,679	2,025	2,510	3,867
of Charges iled by Males	3.60 %	3.70 %	4.90 %	4.70 %	5.10 %	4.30 %	5.40 %	6.00 %	5.90 %
ettlement s	,676	,568	,692	,783	,646	,471	,458	,571	,525

Above are the Numbers of Reported Cases with EEOC 2000-2008 (e)

15%	Males average
85%	Females average
14,390	11% receive settlements

Chapter 36

Why is it Both, Sexual Harassment and Prostitution at Work for Women or Men?

To prostitute any person for a business activity of any kind is deplorable to say, to think, or do in our society. Prostituting is not acceptable in our society on any level, with the exception of the several brothels in Nevada where prostitution is legal. Using the term sexual harassment only is putting a candy label on prostitution at work. Many disgraceful supervisors and managers have enjoyed the "sexual harassment" opportunities. These bosses inflict stress and psychological suffering upon thousands of subordinate employees. Today, victims need to understand he or she is being prostituted, if a boss is demanding sexual services because you are being given a payroll check. The boss is using the subordinate's need for income as leverage to demand sexual control, sexual dominance, or sex from the subordinate.

When an employee encounters sexual harassment, hostile-environment harassment, quid pro quo harassment, a favor-for-a-favor harassment, this-for-that harassment, the subordinate employee yields to the sexual request(s), and money or benefits are received for sex is prostitution. The aggressive dominator has displayed power over the victim and the victims are women or females under the age of 18 years of age in many instances. Destroying the victim's integrity, his or her physical well being, and their mental well being are the intent of the sexually hostile aggressors in many situations (9).

Sexual harassment attacks are affecting the young adult workers, much older workers, teenagers, men, and women. The attack is to control, to have sexual dominance over another individual, and to exercise a monetary slavery; when our business system is a free commerce society.

Chapter 37

Just a Candy Label, Sexual Harassment a Boss' Mind Play-Land

I am taking the candy label off. I am saying sexual harassment from a boss using the subordinate's need for income, as leverage for sex is prostituting the employee. Much of my frustration came from being used as a sex business toy, by the boss. No more candy label. Sexual harassment has serious consequences in the court systems of America. Labeling prostitution for just what prostituting is will have a greater negative and legal impact on the careers of the bosses, who are sexual harassers seeking sex from subordinate employees. Sexual harassment at work is the play-land of the mind for many bosses. Now is the time for the sex seeking bosses to be taken off the sex "merry-go-round" positioned on-the-job; called sexual harassment. It is time to communicate some sexual harassment is an operation to prostitute the subordinate employees. A sexual harasser, in the boss' position knows he or she is conveniently obtaining a sex toy, a whore, *(your job description has been changed)* a cheap item at work. Pull the **bed sheets** all the way down and call prostitution, prostitution. The boss is cheapening your human value and cheapening your employment position with sexual harassment activity.

If the sexually harassed employees will say to him or herself honestly, the demand for sex and sex control, which comes from the boss, is an act of **prostituting employees** you will feel empowered. Your frustration and helplessness should begin to turn around into strength. Everyone knows prostitution is wrong. Take the candy label off and see solicitation for sex using a payroll monetary system is also prostituting employees. Do not sale yourself cheap and do not let others cheapen you. This book is for me and this book is for you. Welcome to the 21st century! It is time to empower the subordinate employees. We have taken a beating from bosses dispensing out sexual harassment.

When Sexual Harassment Feels Like Prostitution

Employees, who have been sexually harassed, have fewer defenses to fight sexual harassment. Keep your head up high and your shoulders back because I did that dealing with sexual harassment for over a decade. You have to have inner strength in dealing with deplorable deeds thrown at you. Some bosses want to take the sparkle out of your eyes, fill your life with stress, and sleepless nights. Share this book at work. The bosses will know you are no longer ignorant to the game of payroll prostitution. Sexual harassment is not just discrimination it's prostitution in some cases.

Chapter 38

Sexual Harassment is No Game; A Battle Launched from the Boss' Chair

---

This book is great tool to help prepare young people for the pit falls in the workplace. The young, the older working employees, males or females all need to read this book. This book is a small tool to help you understand you are not alone and the sexual harassment battle is not your fault. Enjoy taking care of yourself and go to work in your personal best. Remember to do the things that make you happy. Hit the gym, take a walk at lunch, take the kids and the dog out more; just do whatever makes you feel good as a person. Your choice for a mate and friends are not for your boss to place his or her SEX seal of approval on. You can keep a copy of this book in a tote bag or in your car. I know sexual harassment pressure at work is horrible. Please put your name here, keep your personal values high, and keep your head up high. Do not become one of the statistics the boss forces into bed. Do not become trapped by sex controlling behavior coming from the boss' office. Now, this book is for you. Sign your name stating:

> *I Will Not Allow a Boss to Prostitute Me,*
> Signed *Jacqueline Lafayette*

I will not say yes to sexual harassment, sex demands, or sex controlling actions from any boss.

Sign your name: _____

We are not done, please continue reading. Your self confidence should improve even more, as you finish this book.

Chapter 39

Debate an Argument:

Why are the colors **blue** and **cobalt** still in the blue family?

Why are the colors **green** and **lime** still in the green family?

Why is sex for a payment on **any street corner** and sex for a payment on **any job** in the prostitution family?

What is your payroll check for?

When Sexual Harassment Feels Like Prostitution

Money paying for a sex act anywhere is prostitution. Some places in Nevada the business of prostitution is legal. The sex hustling boss demoted his or her subordinate employee's professional role at work. Please, remember the boss' hat is still on his or her head when he or she is demanding sex.

Employees need money to live on. So, why are the bosses prostituting employees? Some sexual harassment is the boss' slick prostitution business on-the-job hustling sex from subordinate employees. The spot light and burden belongs 180 degrees back on the bosses hustling for "sex control or sex" on-the-job, which the supervisor and manager was NOT HIRED for at any company here in the United States. The boss voluntarily changed his or her "paid management role" of responsibility to INCLUDE demanding sex or sex control from the subordinate employee(s). The boss is not in love with the subordinate employee in exercising sex control tactics or payroll payments for sex. Document everything the sexual harassing boss does to you.

Chapter 40

Boss Harassment

The leadership, who voluntarily takes the low-life seat for sex hustling his or her subordinate employee, is in total control or his or her future. If the laws change to help subordinate employees more, we needed that help decades ago.

Men and women, both face sexual harassment, one leading form of discrimination. All too often, the confrontations of sexual harassment are coming from the bosses. Some people, who are supposed to be the leaders and the head administrators at work to provide direction are not living up to boss' obligation to the workers he or she had employed. Some bosses are partaking in deplorable, offensive, and intolerable actions against his or her employees (10).

Chapter 41

Questions, Definitions, and My Conclusion

---

*Why are some bosses demanding **sex** from his or her subordinate employees? Why are some bosses wanting sex favors, due to he or she distributes a **payroll check**? Why are some bosses using his or her company's facility to demand sexual attention? Why are bosses **half** of the sexual harassment problem?*

Why are some sexual harassment encounters at work and prostitution on any street corner are the same?

Some answers are found in Merriam – Webster's Definitions.

Solicit (a)

"1 **a :** to make petition to : entreat

b : to approach with a request or plea

2   : to urge (as one's cause) strongly

3 **a :** to entice or lure especially into evil

b : to proposition (someone) especially as or in the character of a prostitute

4   : to try to obtain by usually urgent requests or pleas"

Prostitute (b)

"1 : to offer indiscriminately for sexual intercourse especially for money

2 : to devote to corrupt or unworthy purposes : debase" (b)

Debase (c)

"1   : to lower in status, esteem, quality, or character" (c)

Sexual Harassment (d)

"1   : uninvited and unwelcome verbal or physical behavior of a sexual nature especially by a person in authority toward a subordinate (as an employee or student)" (d).

MY CONCLUSION: No more **candy label**; illegal sexual harassment is also **illegal prostitution** in some situations, by the defining acts of exchanging sex for money. This person-to-person illegal-candy store is a very expensive legal battle in the court systems. It is time for transparency from company management. I believe the term, goodwill ambassadors, describes an open door to discuss these problems and suggest assistance to provide help that is needed. I have stepped up to begin the negotiation process for the countless victims of sexual harassment to help mediate better futures for all. What a lovely picture, if the Human Resources departments around the world are now able save more careers of the sexually harassed victims and save their companies more millions at the same time. Saving the careers of both, the adults and the teenagers, by the thousands, will put a smile on everyone's face. If the adults working need an ambassador, our teenagers are suffering even greater.

When Sexual Harassment Feels Like Prostitution, Sexual Harassment Is!

(a) Merriam-Webster, Incorporated, Solicit, (2009), www.merriam- webster.com/dictionary/solicit

(b) Merriam-Webster, Incorporated, Prostitute, (2009), www.merriam-webster.com/dictionary/prostitute

(c) Merriam-Webster, Incorporated, Debase, (2009), www.merriam-webster.com/dictionary/debase

(d) Merriam-Webster, Incorporated, Sexual harassment, (2009), merriam-webster.com/dictionary/sexual_ harassment

(e) U.S. Equal Employment Opportunity Comission, www.eeoc.gov/eeoc/statistics/enforcement/sexual_ harassment_new/ (2009)